A PAMPHLET OF ANECDOTES,
PRAISE, SCRIPTURES,
AND THANKSGIVING

Testimonials

OF A

Loving God

SANDRA AITCHESON

I dedicate this book to the Lord of my life, Jesus Christ. I would also like to thank my family for their unending support of love and encouragement in my journey through life. A special thanks also goes to my brother in Christ, Patrick L.C. Meade, who has worked tirelessly to help make this book possible. I praise God for everyone who has held me up in prayer.

Introduction

Life can be very unpredictable, to say the least.

From day to day, anything unexpected can happen, and sometimes we don't know where to turn. All of us at one point in our life can use a word of encouragement to help lift us up. I find that the best source of encouragement is from the Word of God. He has a word of knowledge for every situation and obstacle we face, and who better to turn to than the Creator and Sustainer of all life?

In this devotional, I pray that you will find an answer or guidance for whatever you need. Blessings on your life.

"I will destroy the wisdom of the wise; the intelligence of the intelligent I will frustrate."

—1 CORINTHIANS 1:19 (NIV)

WE ARE ALL united by the Word of God, our belief that Jesus Christ is the Son of God, and the message He preached. The message of the cross is foolishness to those who are perishing, but to us who are saved, it is the power of God. For God said, "I will destroy the wisdom of the wise; the intelligence of the intelligent I will frustrate." God was pleased through the foolishness of what was preached to save those who believe.

For the foolishness of God is wiser than human wisdom, and the weakness of God is stronger than human strength. In the world, God chose foolish things to shame the wise and weak things to shame the strong, so that no one may boast of their own doings and strength. So, let anyone who boasts of anything, boast of the Lord, and the power of His might.

PRAYER

Thank you, Lord, that we attain unto your wise counsel, and learn wisdom through your Word. Amen.

"I have been crucified with Christ and I no longer live, but Christ lives in me. The life I now live in the body, I live by faith in the Son of God, who loved me and gave himself for me."

—GALATIANS 2:20 (NIV)

SOMETHING WONDERFUL HAPPENS inside of us when Christ becomes the Lord of our life. It is no longer we who live, but Christ who lives in us, that is the center of our very being. And we give praise to the Father of all compassion and comfort, who is there for us in times of trouble, that what we've received from Him, can be used to help others. We are transformed, into a new creation that turns to God and His Holy Spirit for every righteous and faith filled move we make.

We can boast with a clear conscience that we have conducted ourselves with the people we've encountered, with integrity and godly sincerity, because we don't rely on worldly wisdom, but on God's grace. We can always be confident of one thing; that God is faithful and in Him our speech will be "Yes" and "Amen," because it is God who makes us stand firm in Christ. He has anointed us, set His seal of ownership on us, and put His Spirit in our hearts as a deposit guaranteeing what is to come, our inheritance in His kingdom.

PRAYER

Thank you, Lord, that we can rely on you and your Holy Spirit, to direct us to where you want us to go. Amen.

"For the word of the LORD is right, and all His work is done in truth. He loves righteousness and justice; the earth is full of the goodness of the LORD."

—PSALM 33:4-5

"BY THE WORD of the Lord the Heavens were made, their starry host by the breath of His mouth" (Psalm 33, verse 6). Can anyone of us say what are God's limitations? Or can we understand or explain the mysteries of the Almighty? They are higher than the Heavens above, and deeper than the depths below. If measured it is longer than the Earth, and wider than the sea. God is all powerful and is able to do anything He wants that is not in contrast to His divine nature. He sees the good that His people do and is pleased. And surely, He recognizes deceivers, and when He sees evil doesn't He take note of that also?

From Heaven, the Lord looks down and sees all mankind, from His dwelling place He watches all who live on Earth, He forms the hearts of all and considers everything that we do. The eyes of the Lord are on those who fear Him, those who put their hope in His never-ending love, He delivers us from death and keeps us alive in days of trouble. There is no one that is mightier than our God.

PRAYER

We praise you Lord, for the work of your hands and the goodness in all the Earth. Amen.

3

║ *"A man's heart plans his way, but the Lord directs his steps."*

— PROVERBS 16:9

HAVE YOU EVER thought that you were in the right place, at the right time? Or couldn't go where you wanted, because of some unforeseen circumstance? Those who accept Jesus as their Lord and Savior, has been blessed with a precious gift from God, His Holy Spirit. And God's Spirit is always with us, guiding our thoughts and even our prayers. But more times than a few, our plans have been changed and we've been sent in a direction we normally wouldn't go.

Maybe there is a traffic jam and we have to go another route but whatever the case we have no control where the Spirit leads us. It could be that we're being moved out of harm's way, or placed where we can help or be a blessing to someone else. We are God's children, and where He leads us, we will go. "A man's heart plans his way, but it's the Lord who directs his steps" (Proverbs 16:9). We are available for God to use as He sees fit, but it's our Lord who receives the glory.

PRAYER

Lord, thank you for your Spirit that leads us in the direction we need to go. Amen.

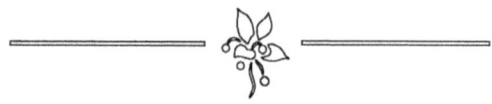

4

"For God so loved the world that He gave His only begotten Son, that whoever believes in Him should not perish but have everlasting life."

—JOHN 3:16

CHRISTMAS HAS ALWAYS been one of the most celebrated times of the year. Midtown Manhattan would be bustling with people shopping and looking at the Christmas displays in the windows. Rockefeller Plaza with its massive tree highlighting the skating rink below. And there was an atmosphere of joy that was indescribable.

You could hear Christmas carols playing and smell the chestnuts that were roasting by vendors in the streets. Everyone was looking for that White Christmas that Bing Crosby would sing about. As much as we loved the lights and Christmas displays, we always remembered the reason we felt so much joy, celebrating the birth of our Lord and Savior, Jesus Christ. And even though it has been thousands of years since Christ's birth, it is still the most wonderful time of the year, because we have a God who stepped out of His glory to bring His light into our lives. I think that's an excellent reason to celebrate.

PRAYER

Thank you, Jesus, for the joy we experience from your miraculous birth. Amen.

"Every good and perfect gift is from above, coming down from the Father of the heavenly lights, who does not change like shifting shadows."

—JAMES 1:17 (NIV)

THE SPIRIT OF discernment is something that I've rarely heard talked about in church. By the dictionary definition: it is the ability to grasp and comprehend what is obscure; it is an act of perceiving. In Christian faith, it is a gift of wisdom, given by the Holy Spirit for us to determine the fruit of one's spirit or a place (whether it is good or evil) and knowing right from wrong. We can ask our heavenly Father for the gift of discernment, which is also known as godly wisdom and like everything else, He will freely give it to us, because it enhances our spiritual life.

Many of us already have a discerning spirit, and don't even realize it. How many times have you met someone, and known right away that they have evil intents? Or how many times have you walked into a place, and felt that you had to leave, because you just had a bad feeling about being there? That's having a discerning spirit, placed in you by the Holy Spirit. Every gift given by our Father is useful, and for our well-being.

PRAYER

Father, thank you for giving us a discerning spirit, to see the fruits of the spirit. Amen.

6

"Truly I tell you, whatever you did for one of the least of these brothers and sisters of mine, you did for me."

—MATTHEW 25:40

SO MUCH HAS changed in the past ten months.* It's difficult to imagine things ever being normal again. So many of our people have lost their income because shops have closed, and lines for soup kitchens and pantries are getting longer every day. No one is ashamed to say that they're hungry and have no food to eat. But there's something powerful about the love of God, that once it's in your heart, you don't think about yourself but putting the needs of others ahead of your own, becomes a priority.

As the body of Christ, we're not concerned with our own physical well-being, because we walk by faith, and are covered by the blood of the Lamb, inside and out. It's a sobering and humbling thought when we see people cooking, feeding and clothing others they've never met before, and not looking for anything in return. These past months has brought out the best in people, that could only have come from the love of God, and it should be this way all the time, not just when tragedy comes.

PRAYER

Thank you, Lord, that we have a heart like yours, full of love for all people. Amen.

* Written during the COVID-19 pandemic in 2020

*"A soft answer turns away wrath, but
a harsh word stirs up anger."*

—PROVERBS 15:1

THERE ARE A lot of Christians in the world, but there are also a lot of people who are not. And the ones who are not, tend to put Christians under a microscope and analyze everything that we do. The way we walk, dress, speak and eat is watched to see if we are just Sunday Christians, or if we are the same during the rest of the week. We have to carry the Spirit of God with us 24/7 and not be drawn into any situation that may cause us to forget who we really belong to.

There are so many in the world who have never experienced the peace and the love of God and will get angry when we exhibit a calmness of spirit. That's when the power of the Word of God comes in very handy. God says, "a soft tongue turns away wrath," so what we need to do is let God's Word work on the hearts of man. If we lose control and add fuel to the fire, it will make matters worse and cause more damage. We are children of light, and light will always push darkness back. So, let the light of God shine bright in us, and, with Gods help, we will win souls for His kingdom.

PRAYER

Thank you, that your Word transforms us into children of light, filled with your love. Amen.

8

"Therefore, you are no longer a slave but a son, and if a son, then an heir of God through Christ."

—GALATIANS 4:7

AT ONE TIME we were all in slavery, but not the slavery that we read about in history books. But we were enslaved by the spiritual forces in the world. When the time was right, God sent His Son to redeem us by adoption, because God placed the Spirit of His Son into our hearts, and we are now heirs of the Father and joint heirs with the Son, that we can call on Abba, our Father. But we must hold fast to our inheritance, and to our faith, because the enemy is lurking and he came to steal, kill and destroy. Christ has set us free, and we must continue to run the good race through faith and love.

We must be careful who we allow into our life, to persuade us and try and draw us away from our belief in God. "A little yeast works through the whole batch of dough," and some who are spiritually weak, can be easily persuaded. So, walk by the spirit, and then we won't gratify the desires of the flesh, Because the flesh and the spirit are in constant conflict with each other. So, we must stand firm, and not give in to worldly influence, because we are children of God and children of the light.

PRAYER

Father, we thank you, that the chains have been broken, and we are no longer bound by sin. Amen.

"It shall come to pass that before they call, I will answer; and while they are still speaking, I will hear."

—ISAIAH 65:24

A WORD FROM Jehovah God: "Behold, I create new heavens and a new earth; and the former shall not be remembered or come to mind. But be glad and rejoice forever in what I create; for behold, I create Jerusalem as a rejoicing, and her people a joy . . . The voice of weeping shall no longer be heard in her, nor the voice of crying . . . For as the days of a tree, so shall be the days of My people, and My elect shall long enjoy the work of their hands . . . For they shall be the descendants of the blessed of the LORD, and their offspring with them. It shall come to pass that before they call, I will answer; and while they are still speaking, I will hear. The wolf and the lamb shall feed together, the lion shall each straw like the ox, and dust shall be the serpent's food. And they shall not hurt nor destroy in all My holy mountain" (Isaiah 65:17–19, 22–25).

What a glorious day in a new creation that will be.

PRAYER

Thank you, Lord, for giving us your promise of things to come to all who walk upright before you. Amen.

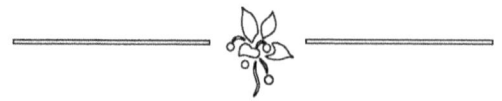

"God is not a man, that He should lie, nor a son of man, that He should repent. Has He said, and will He not do? Or has He spoken, and will He not make it good?"

—NUMBERS 23:19

OUR SOVEREIGN LORD says: "As surely as I live, I take no pleasure in the death of wicked people. I only want them to turn from their wicked ways so that they can live." God's Word is truth. He is not a man that lies, and if He says a thing that's exactly what He means. His Word will not return to Him void but will accomplish all that He's sent it to do. He tells us: "If my people who are called by my name, would humble themselves and pray and seek My face, and turn from their wicked ways, then I will hear from Heaven and I will forgive their sin, and heal the land."

God doesn't ask things that are impossible for us to do, He is loving and merciful. He knows our frame and remembers that we were made from dust. He has forgiven us so many times, sent His only Son to be tortured and die for us, so that we can have a hope of a future with Him. So, pray more and worry less, because the more we pray, is the closer we'll get to God.

PRAYER

We praise you that your Word, Lord, will not return to you void, but will accomplish all that you have sent it to do. Amen.

> *"Blessed be the name of God forever and ever,*
> *for wisdom and might are His. And He changes*
> *the times and the seasons; He removes kings and*
> *raises up kings; He gives wisdom to the wise And*
> *knowledge to those who have understanding."*

—DANIEL 2:20–21

PRAISE BE TO the name of God for ever and ever, wisdom and power are His. He changes times and seasons; He deposes kings and raises up others. He gives wisdom to the wise and knowledge to the discerning. He reveals deep and hidden things, He knows what lies in darkness, and light dwells with Him. I thank and praise you, God of my ancestors. You have given us wisdom and power, you make known to us whatever we ask of you, and you make known to us the deep and hidden things.

When our prayers of faith go up before God's Throne of Grace, He sees what is in our heart, and as long as we believe, our prayers will be answered. We need our hearts to be cleaned by the power of God's Word, so that our prayers will be effective and fervent, and avail much.

PRAYER

We thank you and praise you, O God, because you have given us wisdom and power through your Word. Amen.

"In the beginning God created the Heavens and the Earth. The earth was without form, and void; and darkness was on the face of the deep."

—GENESIS 1:1-2

THERE ARE SO many people in this world who know that there is a God in Heaven, but if you were to ask them who this God is, they wouldn't be able to tell you anything about Him. People know the name of Jesus, the stories of His birth, and even that He was crucified and risen from the dead. But in-between His birth and His death there is a lack of knowledge.

We go to church, and we read the scriptures because we have a hunger to know more about the God we serve. We live in a natural world; we see things with our natural eyes, and we have ears that hear from a natural perspective. We can think and reason logically, but it can only be done with our natural senses. But the God we worship, there is nothing that is natural about Him. He is a Supreme Supernatural God, that will give us an understanding to climb into a higher realm and meet Him on a supernatural level, and there is so much more we can experience, if we just ask Him.

PRAYER

Thank you for teaching us to see beyond our natural senses and experience your power through your Word. Amen.

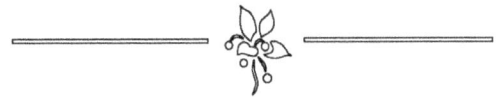

13

The Lord your God is with you, the Mighty Warrior who saves. He will take great delight in you; in His love He will no longer rebuke you but will rejoice over you with singing.

—ZEPHANIAH 3:17 (NIV)

THE LORD OUR God is in our midst, a victorious warrior. He will exult over us with joy, He will be quiet in His love, He will rejoice over us with shouts of joy. Because we are a chosen people, a royal priesthood, a holy nation, God's special possession, that we may declare the praises of Him who called us out of darkness into His wonderful light. So now, our God, listen to the prayer your servants and to our supplications, and for your sake, O Lord, let your face shine on us and be gracious to us. Because the Lord is near to all who call on Him, to all who call on Him in truth. The Lord is rich in mercy and full of grace and strong. The Lord Almighty says, "Not by might, nor by power, but by My Spirit."

So, let's walk led by the path God sets us on.

PRAYER

Thank you for hearing our prayers and making your face to shine on us with your favor. Amen.

"For in Him we live and move and have our being, as also some of your own poets have said, 'For we are also His offspring.'"

—ACTS 17:28

THE GOD WHO made the world and everything in it, is the Lord of Heaven and Earth. He is not waited on and served by human hands, as if He needed us to tend to all of His needs. But rather, He Himself gives everyone life and breath, and everything else that is needed. From Abraham and his seed, He made all the nations of the whole Earth. God made it so no matter where we were, we can reach out, seek Him and find Him, even though He us never far from us. "For in God we live, move and have our very being."

We are His offspring, and we're created in His image. He made us, and not we ourselves, and it is not the other way around. God is a Spirit and is Divine and can't be molded into an image made by human hands. We all must repent of everything that we have done that has offended God. Because there will come a day when we will all be judged, by the one He has appointed whom He rose from the dead, Jesus the Christ.

PRAYER

Thank you, Almighty God, for transforming us into your image, so we will be more like you. Amen.

"This righteousness is given through faith in Jesus Christ ... for all have sinned and fall short of the glory of God."

—ROMANS 3:22–23

I'M QUITE SURE that we all have prayed and repented of our sins, standing before God's Throne of Grace. But do we really know what it means to have a repentant heart, so that our sins can be thrown into the sea of forgetfulness? We all have sinned, and fallen short of God's glory, but to recognize our shortcomings that causes us to sin, and repent of them, is asking God to remove them as far as the east is from the west and not repeat those sins. Sin isn't only something that we physically do, but it can be a thought, word or a deed.

Every day we wake up, we are confronted with sins, not by our own doing, but because of the world we live in. The enemy is lurking around waiting to bombard us with anything, that will take our mind off of the God we serve. That's why it is so important to stay rooted and grounded in the Word of God. He is our only hope and salvation.

PRAYER

Father, we thank you that we are cleansed and washed of all unrighteousness. Amen.

"Heaven and Earth will pass away, but My Words will by no means pass away. But of the day and hour no one knows, not even the angels of Heaven, but My Father only."

—MATTHEW 24:35-36

WE HAVE LIVED long enough in this world to know how to prepare in the event of coming disaster. If a hurricane is predicted, we secure windows, get our kerosene lamps out and stock up on food supplies. Even during this pandemic, we knew what to do to make sure our cupboards wouldn't be empty. So, it's the same way we must be prepared and ready, because Jesus will come at an hour and time when no one will expect Him.

That day or hour no one knows, not even the angels in Heaven, or the Son, but only the Father. People will be going about their business as usual, and not be aware of when Christ returns, until two men will be standing together and one will be taken, and the other one left. If we knew ahead of time what was going to happen, we would be on our P's and Q's and would always be ready. Christ will come like a thief at night, keep watchful so we won't be left behind. Blessings and love.

PRAYER

Thank you, Jesus, for the instruction in your Word to keep us alert and ready for your return. Amen.

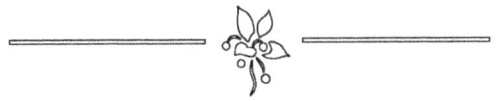

"If we confess our sins, He is faithful and just and will forgive us our sins and purify us from all unrighteousness."

—1 JOHN 1:9 (NIV)

CONFESSING OUR SINS to God can make the biggest difference in our life. God is Faithful and Just and will honor His promises. Nothing can wash away our sins and make us right with God, only Jesus can do that. Then we will be blessed because our transgressions are forgiven and our sins covered. "Blessed is the one whose sin the Lord does not count against them and in whose spirit is no deceit" (Psalm 32:2).

When we don't repent of our sins, the Lord's hand is heavy on us, and we groan day and night because our strength is sapped. So, remain faithful in prayer, because the Lord is our hiding place and our deliverance. He will teach us the way we should go, and counsel us with His loving eye on us. God wants to give us a clean heart and a right spirit, so we can in truth be called the children of God.

PRAYER

Thank you, Father, for delivering us from sin and shame, and cleansing us of all unrighteousness. Amen.

"All the angels stood around the throne and the elders and the four living creatures, and fell on their faces before the throne and worshiped God."

—REVELATION 7:11

ARE ANGELS REAL?

If you were to take a survey, almost everyone asked would say, definitely yes. In our minds eye we perceive angels to be heavenly beings with beautiful wings flowing from their backs, who move around doing the will of our Father. The word *angel* means messenger, and we have Gabriel, who delivers messages from God, and Michael, a warrior angel, who is dispatched to fight and do the will of the Father. God created angels, before He created anything else in the universe, and they praise and worship God around His Throne. And if you can imagine a ladder, with angels descending and ascending according to the words we speak, because they minister to all who believe in Christ.

I've heard it said that we all have an angel assigned to us. And I believe that it is because we are that important to God. And isn't there always someone there to help us when we need it? Angels play a role in Heaven, just like we have assignments here on Earth, and it's all for the glory of God.

PRAYER

Lord, I thank you, that you dispatch your angels to help us in times of need. Amen.

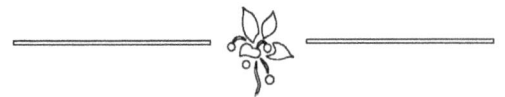

"'For My thoughts are not your thoughts, nor are your ways My ways,' says the Lord."

—ISAIAH 55:8

WE WILL NEVER forget the story of Adam and Eve, because it speaks to our present situation. But what is equally important, is the story of Cain and Abel. After Cain killed his brother, God banished him and sent him out into the world. But Cain was afraid that he would constantly be attacked because of what he did to Abel. But God marked Cain with a sign of His protection, so no one would take revenge on him. This act tells us of the depth of God's love and the mercies He has toward us.

If any of us were to commit murder, our present judicial system would put us in jail probably for the rest of our life. But God's ways are not our ways, and His thoughts can't be compared to the way we think. This is a perfect example to show us that no sin is too great, that we can't be forgiven by our Father because of His unconditional love. That's where Jesus steps in, because He is the gateway to our forgiveness.

PRAYER

Thank you, Lord, that your mercies extend beyond what we deserve. Amen.

"For God is not the author of confusion, but of peace, as in all churches of the Saints"

—1 CORINTHIANS 14:33

WE ALL FACE uncertainties in our life. We go to bed at night, and none of us knows what tomorrow will bring. We can make a list of things that we plan to do for the day, and how much time is needed to complete it. And when something unexpected pops up, it throws our plans into disarray, and we have to make adjustments. But when we consult God before we do anything, you can be sure things will run smoothly.

Because "A man's heart plans his way, but the Lord directs his steps" (Proverbs 16:9). God's peace will keep your mind from worry because; God is not a God of confusion, but of peace. So, get into the habit of praying first, and asking God to help you accomplish all you have to do in the day, and He'll be more than happy to help you.

PRAYER

Thank you, Lord, that we turn to you for the best advice possible, so our paths will be blessed. Amen.

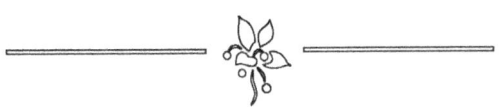

> *"Therefore, go and make disciples of all nations, baptizing them in the name of the Father and of the Son and of the Holy Spirit."*

—MATTHEW 28:19 (NIV)

WE ALL HAVE a responsibility to spread the gospel that Christ taught us to every corner of the Earth. Jesus said: "Therefore go and make disciples of all nations, baptizing them in the name of the Father, and of the Son, and of the Holy Spirit." This was known as the Great Commission, and Christ wants us to grow in faith, as we learn what He taught, so we in turn, can become disciples of God.

Notice, that Christ gave a command for us to reach everyone, everywhere. It wasn't an option, if we wanted to go or not. When we learn the truth about God and His kingdom, we must become an extension of God and share with everyone the knowledge of Christ. It's important that we absorb what we are taught, but it is equally important that we be doers, and not just hearers. Before Christ returns, everyone on the face of this Earth will come to know the name of Jesus, and blessed are those who accept Him as the Son of God.

PRAYER

Father, let all that you've taught us be used to spread the gospel of Jesus. Amen.

"Each of you should use whatever gift you have received to serve others, as faithful stewards of God's grace in its various forms."

—1 PETER 4:10 (NIV)

GOD HAS GIVEN each one of us gifts or talents that are used to encourage other people or bring out the best in ours and their lives. God equips us with what we need, when we use our God given talents to help people. Jesus, who was the best at whatever He did, when He walked the Earth, had a special gift of communicating with ordinary people, so that they could easily understand His teachings. He used parables to tell a story that they could relate to.

Until Christ came, the only connection people had to God's Word was from the temple priests, who gave them limited knowledge so they could maintain control over the masses. But Jesus let all people know that the kingdom, and the Word of God, was available to all who received Christ as the Son of God. The same is true for yesterday, today and tomorrow.

PRAYER

Thank you, Lord, for gifts you have given us, to be used for the glory of your holy name. Amen.

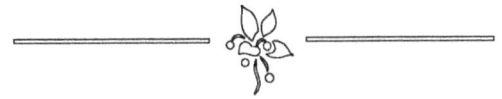

Now after six days Jesus took Peter, James, and John . . . on a high mountain by themselves; and He was transfigured before them . . .And behold, Moses and Elijah appeared to them, talking with Him.

MATTHEW 17:1-3

I USED TO think that once we passed on, and our spirits returned to God, that there was no way they could come back to the Earthly realm. But after being encouraged by scriptures that I've read, I've had to change my opinion on that thought. At the Transfiguration, didn't Moses and Elijah come back and talk with the Son of God? And didn't Saul summon Samuel back from the dead?

I've learned not to put God in a box and limit His power. When our loved ones have passed on, and our hearts are crying out in pain, God can send us what we need to bring us comfort. And sensing the presence of a loved one, knowing that they are right there beside us, is one way God comforts us, to show the extent of His love for us. Blessings and love.

PRAYER

Father, we thank you for the depth of your comfort and abiding love you have for us. That we not only feel your presence, but the presence of our loved ones who have gone on before. Amen.

‖ *"How lovely is your dwelling place, Lord Almighty!"*

PSALM 84 PAINTS a beautiful picture of life in the kingdom of God. We have something amazing to look forward to:

How lovely is your dwelling place, Lord Almighty. Our soul yearns, even faints for the courts of the Lord. Our hearts and our flesh cry out for the living God. Even the sparrow has found a home near your altar, our God and our King. Blessed are those who dwell in your house, they are forever praising you. Hear our prayer, Almighty God, look with favor on your anointed ones, and blessed are those who put their strength in you. Better is one day in your courts than a thousand elsewhere, because we would rather be a doorkeeper in your house, than to dwell in the tents of wickedness. For the Lord God bestows favor and honor, and no good thing will He withhold whose walk is blameless before Him.

PRAYER

We praise you, Lord, for in you we put our trust and wait for an eternity to spend with you. Amen.

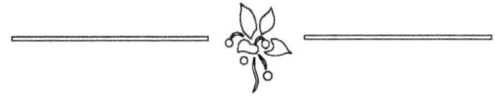

"Love your enemies, bless those who curse you."

—MATTHEW 5:44

ONE OF THE most difficult things to do, for any human being, is to show genuine love and compassion for people who don't care one thing about you. But how people feel about you shouldn't take away from the love of God that is inside of you. The way they feel is something they have to overcome, and that is done by developing a relationship with God. We can't force people to feel the same way we do, but we serve a God Who can turn hearts any which way He wills.

Matthew 5, verse 44 says, "Love your enemies, bless those who curse you, do good to those who hate you, and pray for those who spitefully use you and persecute you." Jesus says, "If someone slaps you on one cheek, turn to them the other also. Give to everyone who ask you, and if anyone takes what belongs to you, do not demand it back. Do to others as you would have them do to you. Be merciful, as our Father is merciful" (Luke 6, verses 29–31, 36).

PRAYER

Thank you, Father, for teaching us to show mercy to others, as you have had mercy on us. Amen.

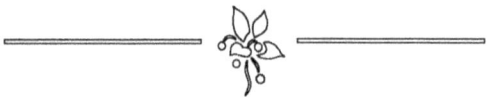

‖ *"Let us make man in our image."*

GOD WANTS US to hold fast to the only hope we have, Jesus Christ, for our healing, our deliverance, our peace, joy and salvation. Because of our inheritance from Adam, we have been born tainted by sin, and our only way out is a cleansing and washing by the sacrificial blood of Jesus.

Genesis 1:26 says, *"Let us make man in our image."* Can you tell me any part of God that is sick, infirmed, afflicted or not perfect? So, if we are made in the image of God, we should be walking in the light and the perfection that God created us. Throughout our lifetime we have heaped abuses on our body, that with age has caused it to break down. But we have a God that knows our frame and remembers that we are dust. We an intercessor that feels everything we're going through and responds to our cries for mercy. God's love has given us salvation, hope and eternal life through Jesus.

PRAYER

Thank you, Lord, that you created us, and understand our weaknesses. Amen.

"Let us not judge one another . . . but rather resolve this, not to put a stumbling block or a cause to fall in our brother's way."

—ROMANS 14:13

THERE ARE TRAIN engineers that put their trust in the mechanics to make sure that the tracks are straight with no kinks in it. Our life can be equated to a train and track also. Sometimes we run around and get off track, but we always manage to know how to get back on with a little help from others.

Are we our brother's keeper?

Yes, we are.

We were commanded to love one another as Christ loves us. But it is not only by words, but by our actions also. If we truly love someone, shouldn't we want what is best for them at all times? It is our responsibility to keep on eye on our brothers and sisters so that they don't lose that precious gift given us by God's grace—salvation. If we see a foot being turned out of joint, we have to do our best to put it back in place or we might find ourselves being held accountable for not even trying to set someone back on the right track. Salvation is free, but we have to do our best to make sure it's available to all.

PRAYER

Thank you, Lord, that you have given us a heart to care for other salvation, as well as our own. Amen.

"God will repay each person according to what they have they have done."

—ROMANS 2:6 (NIV)

GOD IS NOT a respecter of persons, and He doesn't show favoritism. Romans 2:6–8 tells us, "God will repay each person according to what they have done. To those by persistence and doing good, seek glory, honor and immortality, he will give eternal life. But for those who are self-seeking and reject the truth, and follow evil, there will be wrath and anger" (NIV).

There will be trouble and distress for every human being who does evil, but glory, honor and peace for everyone who does good. All who sin apart from the law, will also perish apart from the law, and all who sin under the law will be judged by the law. For it is not those who hear the law who are righteous in God's sight, but those who obey the law who will be declared righteous. We must be doers of the Word, and not just hearers, and put into practice what we have learned; and our hearts will be sealed unto God by His Holy Spirit.

PRAYER

Teach us to put into action what your Word has taught us. Amen.

"We are not trying to please people but God, who tests our hearts. You know we never used flattery, nor did we put on a mask to cover up greed—God is our witness.

—1 THESSALONIANS 2:4-6 (NIV)

IT'S VERY EASY to flatter people, tell them what they want to hear, and just go along to get along with whatever they're doing. But what does that profit us anything. We weren't placed on this Earth to glorify people, but in everything we do it's to be pleasing in the sight of God.

We should never be ashamed of the gospel of Jesus Christ, to declare His Word to all who will listen, because it's for their eternal life and salvation. Our lives should be an open book, because we are witnessing by our actions as well as our words, for us to be encouraging and comforting as we live worthy of God and called into His glorious kingdom.

PRAYER

Thank you for giving us a heart, Lord, that pursues after you. Amen.

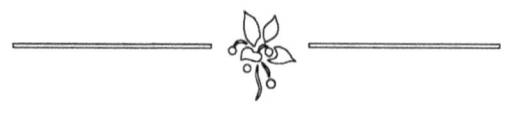

"Their feet rush into sin . . . they pursue evil schemes."

—ISAIAH 59:7 (NIV)

HAVE YOU EVER rushed to do something, knowing it was the wrong thing to do, but went ahead and did it anyway? Hasty steps and feet can lead you down a path of destruction. We walk along crooked paths, and then wonder why we can't find any peace. Isaiah 59, verse 7 says that *their feet rush into sin, and they pursue evil schemes.* Our iniquities have separated us from our God, and our sins have hidden His face from us, so He will not hear. Justice and righteousness are far from us and does not reach us. But still, we look for a bright light, blindly groping along a wall to find our way, but all is darkness. "The arm of the Lord is not too short to save, nor his ear too dull to hear" (Isaiah 59, verse 1).

His compassion and love are always there to guide us through. Seek the Lord while He may be found and call on His name while He is near to you, and the Lord will have mercy on you.

PRAYER

We praise you, Lord, that your compassion and love never fails. Amen.

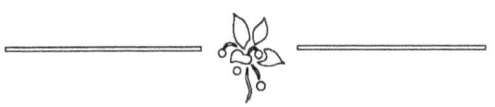

31

| *"The Lord is my portion: therefore, I will wait for Him."*

—LAMENTATIONS 3:24 (NIV)

WE WERE CREATED to Praise God. There is no better way to start our day than with Praise on our lips, and Thanksgiving in our hearts to Glorify the God of all creation. Lamentations 3:24 says, "The Lord is my portion; therefore, I will wait for Him" (NIV). The Lord is good to those who's hope us in Him, to the one who seeks Him. When we Praise the Lord with shouts of joy and victory resounds, Psalm 118, verse 16 says, "The Lord's right hand has done mighty things" (NIV). We have all heard the saying, "When praise goes up, the blessings come down."

Believe it!

As Christians we have experienced the goodness of our Lord, more times than a few.

God will never see His children forsaken, or His seed begging bread. No good thing will the Lord withhold from those who walk upright before Him. Our praise and glory to God activates the Word of God in our lives, and God's angels carry His blessings for every word we speak. Praise is a vital part of worship to acknowledge that God is all and everything we need to sustain us, not only here on Earth, but to prepare us for our heavenly destination.

Don't miss out on all God is freely giving to us.

PRAYER

Thank you, Lord, for keeping praise on our lips and thanksgiving in our hearts to worship you.

| *"Blessed be Your glorious name."*

—NEHEMIAH 9:5

IT IS GOOD to give thanks to the Lord, and to praise His glorious name. The moment we open our eyes in the morning, His praise and thanksgiving should be on our lips. There is no one like our God who is worthy. Nehemiah 9, verses 5–7 declares God's might: "Blessed be Your glorious name, which is exalted above all blessing and praise . . . You have made heaven, the heaven of heavens, with all their host, the earth and everything on it, the seas and all that is in them, and You preserve them all. The host of heaven worships You."

You see our sufferings and you hear our cries, but most times in our own arrogance we fail to acknowledge the miracles that you have worked throughout time, and in our lives. But you are a forgiving God, gracious and compassionate, slow to anger and abounding in love. And you have never let go of our hand. You have poured out benefits out on us, and sometimes we don't even recognize that it is your hand that has brought us through. Anoint us with a mind like your Son, that we will always praise your holy name.

PRAYER

Thank you, merciful Lord, that even through our failures, you still hold us up in your righteousness. Amen.

❚ *"I know the plans I have for you."*

—JEREMIAH 29:11 (NIV)

I KNOW SOME people who can take a few ingredients and turn it into an amazingly delicious meal. And then we have the bakers, who can whip butter and sugar that will leave your mouth watering. Well, God has His own recipe that will make our lives just as appealing and beneficial to our soul and spirit. Jeremiah 29:11 says, "I know the plans I have for you . . . to prosper you and not to harm you, plans to give you hope and a future."

God's recipe may include some battles, trials and triumphs, but it all will lead to victory. God's purpose for each of us is for His glory to be revealed in our daily life, to be transformed into the image of His Son, and to share in the inheritance of Christ. We are being molded, and fashioned into who God created us to be, children of the Most High God. Sometimes we have to let go of the reins, and let God do His thing. No one can do it better than He can.

PRAYER

You, Lord, direct our lives, and we will never be lost when we depend on you. Amen.

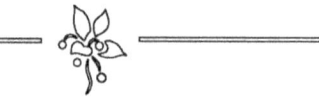

"Your faith should not be in the wisdom of men but in the power of God."

—1 CORINTHIANS 2:5

HOW DEEP DOES your faith run?

Studying Hebrews, the book full of faith walkers, should encourage us to seek God's face and be obedient to His Word. Have what we've learned by reading it changed our way of thinking, to know that a little faith can move mountains and obstacles in our life? From one day to the next, so many things can go wrong and we are searching for a solution to set things right again.

It's in our nature to try and fix things. But God is amazing and all He says is to trust Him, walk in faith and obedience and let Him handle even the smallest things in our life. We have no problem popping a pill in our mouth or doing exactly what the doctor says we should do in order to maintain our health. But we have to remember that God created all things, even the medicine we take comes from God's Earth. So, we should learn to have more faith in our Maker as well.

PRAYER

In you, Lord, we put our faith and trust in your power. Amen.

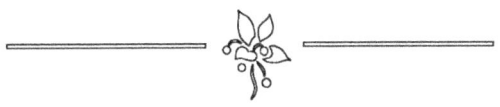

"The god of this age has blinded the minds of unbelievers."

—2 CORINTHIANS 4:4 (NIV)

MANY OF US listen to the radio. And when we turn that radio to a certain frequency we get clarity of what is being said over the airways. That's what we need to do, adjust our spiritual ears to hear God's Holy Spirit speaking to us. One of the best ways I know how is to learn what God is speaking to us through His Word. He gives us a perspective on His wisdom that keeps us focused on His truth, and not on our prideful ways of seeing things.

2 Corinthians 4, verse 4 tells us that the god of this age has blinded the minds of unbelievers, so that they cannot see the light of the gospel which displays the glory of Christ, who is the image of God. God made His light shine in our hearts, to give us a light of the knowledge, displayed in the face of Christ. In Jesus there is no darkness, and once the light of God's Word is in you, darkness cannot exist. Arrogance and pride are two sins we should avoid, because it takes our eyes off of Christ. We have to drown out the noise of this world and meditate day and night to hear clearly God's Spirit.

PRAYER

Thank you for giving us a clarity of vision, and ears to hear what you say. Amen.

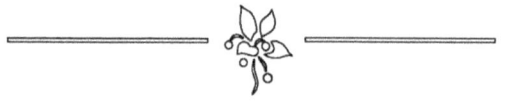

| *"I am the way, the truth, and the life."*

—JOHN 14:6

JESUS CAME TO rescue and to save. He is our only hope for salvation and to see the goodness of God, and all He has prepared for us. Tomorrow may be too late for us to accept this perfect gift from above.

Our sins have earned us and eternal death, but Jesus took our punishment on Himself, we did the sinning, He did the dying. If a building is on fire, and you're standing in the middle of a blazing inferno, and someone comes to rescue you and bring you to safety. Do you say, "No, leave me right here and I'll wait till the flames go out, instead of grabbing hold of the arms that are going to save you?" That wouldn't be very smart. You would cling to your rescuer and never let go.

That's who Jesus is: our deliverer to save us from eternal death. Hold fast to Him and experience His unfailing love.

PRAYER
....

Thank you, Jesus, that you never leave us or abandon us. Amen.

"Love is patient, love is kind."

—1 CORINTHIANS 13:4 (NIV)

IT MAY BE very difficult for any human being to understand the extent of the love that God has for us, His people. We were born into a world that is emotionally fragile, and we wear, as it were, our hearts on our sleeves. We experience hatred, jealousy, pain and love, and sometimes we go a little bit over the top. We feel anger and hold grudges, and most times it's difficult for us to let go, forgive and forget. Imagine, if that's how our God treated us and saw us. 1 Corinthians 13, verse 4 says that God's love is patient and is kind, there's no envy or boasting, and is not proud.

God does not keep a record of any wrongdoing, does not delight in evil but rejoices in truth. It's really kind of hard to understand how we could be loved so unconditionally, because we really don't deserve it. But that is the extent of the love God has for all of His people. God doesn't move whichever way the wind blows, His Word is firm and secure and it never changes. Hold on to God's love and He will never let you go.

PRAYER

Let your light shine in us and drive out all darkness. Amen.

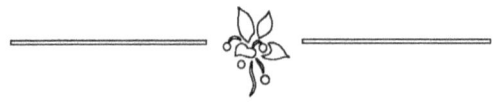

"God, who made the world and everything in it, since He is Lord of heaven and earth, does not dwell in temples made with hands."

—ACTS 17:24

HE IS NOT served by human hands, as if He needed anything. But rather, He Himself gives life and breath and everything else. God did this so that we would seek Him and find Him, though He is never far from anyone of us. We are His offspring and in Him we live move and have our very being.

Our lives completely depend on the Lord God. Our Creator is not an idol, but a spirit and a divine being, and was not fashioned into an image made by human hands. Anyone who worships idols must repent for God will set a day when He judges the world with justice by the one He has appointed by raising Him from the dead. We don't have plenty of time to change our ways because the coming of the Lord is very near.

PRAYER

We praise you, Lord, for there is no God like you in all of creation. Amen.

"They may be called trees of righteousness, the planting of the LORD."

—ISAIAH 61:3

MANY PEOPLE ARE gardeners and can grow just about anything. When you plant a seed, you expect that seed to flourish and grow and produce the crop that is intended. Isaiah 61, verse 3 tells us that we are trees of righteousness, the planting of the Lord, for the display of His splendor. The Spirit of the sovereign Lord is upon us because He has anointed us to proclaim good news to the poor.

We are to tell all people of the Lord's favor, and comfort those who are in need. To provide for all of those who grieve and give them a crown of beauty instead of ashes. The oil of joy for mourning, and a garment of praise for the spirit of heaviness. We will be called priests of the Lord, and ministers of our God. And help restore people and places that have been devastated and ruined. When the Lord waters us and causes us to grow, the work we do for Him will bring glory to His name.

PRAYER

Thank you for keeping us firmly planted in your Word. Amen.

40

"When a man's ways please the Lord, He makes even his enemies to be at peace with him."

—PROVERBS 16:7

WE HAVE SEEN over the course of time how government edicts have removed religion and traces of God from our society, and from the minds of our children. Prayer has been removed from our schools, and it has really changed the way our children think, when God has been taken out of the equation.

BIG MISTAKE.

Why is it so difficult for those in power to see how things have spiraled out of control, when they caused a separation from God with our society? We must remain vigilant and prayerful before God, and the hand of God will never leave us. In Daniel 6; Darius saw that there was no power greater than that of Jehovah God and declared that in his kingdom everyone was to reverence our God. "For He is the living God, and He rescues and He saves" (Daniel 6:27). We need God's saving grace to get us through times like these. We need to pray God's written Word, because the power of God will move when His Word goes into the atmosphere. Prayer changes things, believe it.

PRAYER

Help to maintain an attitude of prayer, to stay connected to you. Amen.

41

"Your word is a lamp to my feet and a light to my path."

—PSALM 119:105

I DON'T KNOW anyone who was born to be a great parent before they had children. This is something that you learn as you go along and get better at it. As our children grow, we realize that they have different personalities, and cannot be treated the same as their siblings. We have to develop great patience, and an understanding of how to encourage them through wisdom developed over the years.

The Bible is the best "go to book," that can help you develop the skills you need to raise up a child with the love of God. Christ Jesus taught us to exercise self-control and a calmness of spirit, in dealing with difficult situations and people. When we read God's Word, we gain more of an insight into the habits of Christ, that becomes very useful in developing our relationships with others. There's so much for us to learn, and it is available to all who want it.

PRAYER

Thank you, Lord, that your Word brings light into my life and gives me guidance. Amen.

"As for you, you meant evil against me;
but God meant it for good."

—GENESIS 50:20

I WAS READING the story of Joseph in Genesis 39 and how his jealous brothers sold him into slavery just to get rid of him. But there is something amazing about the plans of God. Our lifespan on this Earth is just a spot in time when you look at the grand scheme of things. Joseph's life was centered around and focused on God. So, he lived a life that was pleasing to the sight of God.

Even though it was evil what his brothers did, God saw beyond their wickedness and used it for good, to preserve a nation and fulfill promises He made. Most times we don't see down the line, to know where our purpose in life will lead us. But God already knows how we will be used for His glory and accomplish what He needs done. Just know, that God will never take you where He won't protect and sustain you. Be a willing servant, and you will be blessed.

PRAYER

Thank you, Lord, that your plans are better than anything we could do on our own. Amen.

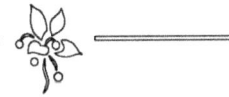

"Therefore, since Christ suffered for us in the flesh, arm yourselves also with the same mind, for he who has suffered in the flesh has ceased from sin."

—1 PETER 4:1

THE BEST EXAMPLE we can follow to obtain a Godly life, is that of Christ Jesus our Lord. As Christians this is what we strive to do, to live a holy and righteous life, so that we can see God. 1 Peter 4:1–2 tells us that we should arm ourselves with the same attitude as Christ because whoever suffers in the body is done with sin. And as a result, we do not live the rest of our earthly lives with evil desires, but rather for the will of God. We have spent enough time fulfilling the desires of the flesh, but when you know better you do better.

Once Christ becomes the central focus of your life we put aside the things that we know are contrary to God's Word. The end of all things is near. Therefore, we should be alert and of a sober mind and always pray. Above all, we should love each other deeply, because love covers a multitude of sins. And if anyone speaks, we should do so as one speaking the very words of God. If we serve others, we should do so with the strength that God provides. So that in all things, God may be praised in all things through Jesus Christ.

PRAYER

Lord, let the words of our mouth and the meditations of our hearts be acceptable in your sight. Amen.

"They will see the Son of Man coming on the clouds of heaven with power and great glory."

—MATTHEW 24:30

WHEN CHRIST JESUS inhabited the Earth, He came as fully man and fully God. He promised, on the third day, He would rise from the dead, and that's exactly what He did. Matthew 24, verse 30 says that we will see the Son of Man coming on the clouds of the sky with power and great glory. Revelations 1:7 says, "He is coming with clouds, and every eye will see Him."

The human side of Jesus suffered and died on the cross, but He arose as King of Kings, and Lord of Lords. Christ will not return until everyone, from every nation, will know the name of Jesus, so that no one can say they don't know who Jesus Christ is. The first time Jesus came it was as a servant, when He comes again it will be as king and judge. "And God has exalted Him to the highest place and given Him a name which is above every name, that at the name of Jesus, every knee shall bow and every tongue confess that Jesus Christ is Lord, to the glory of God the Father" (Philippians 2:9).

PRAYER

Lord, teach us to serve as you did to bring glory to your name. Amen.

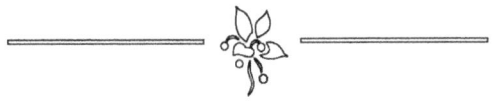

45

‖ "The Lord is a refuge for the oppressed."

—PSALM 9:9 (NIV)

ANYONE WHO LOOKS to the Lord for solutions to whatever situation they are facing, will never have His door closed in their face. And God will give us the best answer and guidance we need. Psalm 9:9–10 (NIV) says: "The Lord is a refuge for the oppressed, a stronghold in times of trouble. Those who know your name trust in you, for you, LORD, have never forsaken those who seek You."

The Lord reigns forever, He has established His throne for judgment. He rules the world in righteousness and judges the people with equity. Sing praises to our God in Zion, because He does not ignore the cries of the afflicted. He has mercy on us and lifts us up that we may rejoice in His salvation. The Lord is known by His acts of justice. He will not forsake the needy and our hope in Him will never die. Praises to the mighty name of our Lord.

PRAYER

Thank you when we cry out to you for help, you hear and answer. Amen.

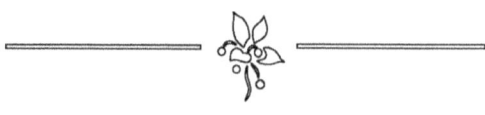

"The one who gets wisdom loves life."

—PROVERBS 19:8 (NIV)

IN THE BIBLE Solomon was deemed a very wise man and wrote many sayings pertaining to wisdom. It wasn't for his own benefit, but for the lives of others, so we could gain a better understanding and avoid foolish things. When we attain unto wise counsel, we avoid traps that would send us in the wrong direction and cause problems in our life. "Listen to advice and accept discipline, and at the end you will be counted among the wise. Many are the plans in a person's heart, but it is the Lord's purpose that prevails" (Proverbs 19:20–21, NIV). "The one who gets wisdom loves life, and the one who cherishes understanding will soon prosper" (Proverbs 19:8, NIV).

Many people are wise in their own way, which is good, but sometimes we all need reminding so that our walk in life will be kept on the right track. "Whoever keeps commandments keeps their life . . . whoever is kind to the poor lends to the LORD, and He will reward them for what they have done" (Proverbs 19:17, NIV).

PRAYER

Thank you that the wisdom of your Word is discipline and life. Amen.

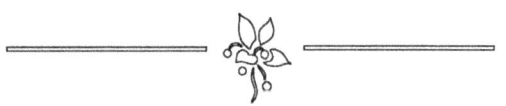

47

"Who redeemed your life from destruction, who crowned you with loving kindness, and tender mercies."

—PSALM 103:4

IT'S MAN'S NATURE to gain and have control over people and situations. We strive to be the best that we can be and want everyone to know it. We are not machines that can operate 24/7 without resting or breaking down. Sometimes, we have to step back and let someone else take charge so we can be refreshed and renewed. Even machines need to have parts replaced or oiled in order for it to work at peak perfection.

Psalm 103 tells us that the Lord has benefits for all who let Him take control of our life. He redeems us from our own destructive ways and satisfies our mouth with good things so that our youth is renewed as the eagles. God is merciful and gracious, and He knows us better than we know ourselves. Even when we cannot see for ourselves that we need to slow down and stop trying to take charge of everything. All the time, God sees it. Somehow or the other, He will pull our coattails and make us rest because of His never-ending love. We need to be still and let the Holy Spirit guide us, and our lives will be much better.

PRAYER

I thank you, Lord, for saving me from my own destructive ways. Amen.

"And behold, there was a great earthquake; for an angel of the Lord descended from heaven, and came and rolled back the stone."

—MATTHEW 28:2

IT IS ONLY fitting and right that we continually celebrate and remember the most glorious day in the Christian year—the Resurrection of our Lord and Savior Jesus Christ. Matthew 28:2–3 says, "And behold, there was a great earthquake; for an angel of the Lord descended from heaven, and came and rolled back the stone from the door, and sat on it. His countenance was like lightning, and his clothing as white as snow." Mark 16:5–6 says that as they approached the tomb, they were told, "Do not be alarmed. You seek Jesus of Nazareth, who was crucified. He is risen! He is not here."

We are sanctified and blessed, because we have a High Priest who intercedes on our behalf. After such a brutal ending to His earthly life, Jesus is seated in all glory at the right hand of Jehovah God, the Father Almighty. Praise His holy name.

PRAYER

Praise you, Lord, that your sacrifice has opened my way for eternal life. Amen.

"Do not boast about tomorrow, for you do not know what a day may bring."

—PROVERBS 27:1 (NIV)

"PROCRASTINATION IS THE thief of time."

Why put off for tomorrow, what you can do today?

We all know things in our life that needs our immediate attention, but most of us will say: "Tomorrow is another day." Proverbs 27:1 says: "Don't boast about tomorrow, for you do not know what a day may bring." Tomorrow is not promised for anyone. We must not brag about our plans or sink our hopes in them. I do know that there is one thing that we should never neglect to do, and that is to keep our eyes focused on Christ Jesus.

Hebrews 2:3 says: "How shall we escape if we ignore so great a salvation?" Jesus didn't just come to earth and sacrifice His life for us because He didn't have anything else better to do. It was because He loves us so much, and we needed His salvation to have eternal life. Let's not put on the sideline what God has blessed us with.

PRAYER

Thank you for blessing us with the gift of salvation. Amen.

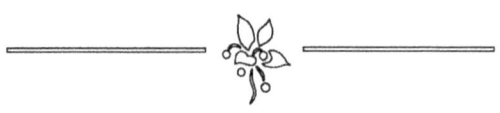

"Blessed are those who have not seen and yet have believed."

—JOHN 20:29

HAVE YOU EVER imagined how you would feel, living in the time when Christ walked the Earth? Two thousand years after Christ's ministry we've learned more about Him, by reading His Word, than we ever could have learned being there with Him. Can you imagine witnessing the miraculous healings that Jesus did? Or sitting and listening to His Sermon on the Mount? John 20:29 says, "Blessed are those who have not seen and yet have believed."

Would we have been one of the ones that believed what Jesus said, and followed Him? Or would we have been in the crowd yelling, "Crucify Him?" Through the Word of God we have been able to see the whole picture: from His birth to His resurrection, and everything in-between. And we can count ourselves more blessed for believing. Blessings and love.

PRAYER

Thank you for giving us your Word to see the miracles of your life. Amen.

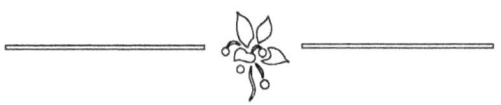

51

> *"For where two or three are gathered together in My name, I am there in the midst of them."*
>
> —MATTHEW 18:20

RECENTLY, I'VE COME across two quotes.

"A family that prays together, stays together."

When the Word of God is the focal point in a household, and family prays and stands in agreement with one another, God is right there in the midst of them, and His power will manifest in that home.

"A world that prays is a world at peace."

We can see by the news reports every day that there is so much division in countries because there isn't unity in prayer. Leaders are trying to grab hold of power to control not only their nation, but other nations as well. They seemed to have forgotten that there is one source and one power in this world, God the good, the omnipotent. Without the peace of God, we are lost.

PRAYER

Father, there is power in prayer and power in agreement through your Word. Amen.

> *"The name of the Lord is a strong tower; the Righteous run to it and are safe."*

—PROVERBS 18:10

DURING THIS PAST year, I believe more people have run to find shelter in the Lord, that they never thought they would do.* Pre-pandemic, so many people were caught up in the bustle of running to work and coming home to take care of the house and the kids that they never had time for anything else. But our focus had to shift when we realized that this pandemic was something greater than what we could handle on our own.

We need a solid foundation to stand on, and the name of Jesus to protect us. We were humbled and brought to our knees and cried out to the God of all creation to save us; I hope that never ends.

PRAYER

Thank you for being our sure foundation that never fails. Amen.

---

* Written during the COVID-19 pandemic in 2020–2021

53

"But do not forget to do good and to share, for with such sacrifices God is well pleased.

—HEBREWS 13:16

I'VE ALWAYS BEEN in the habit of scheduling all of my appointments early. I would get there early and leave at a reasonable time so that I could spend the rest of my day the way I wanted. But then when I really thought about it, I realized that I didn't like being in a crowd of people that I didn't know. But if I want to follow the examples Christ had laid out, I need to shift my way of thinking and be available for as many people as possible. Sometimes, we have to use a different strategy to be in the right place at the right time.

Think of Jesus and the Samaritan woman at the well. Was it an accident that He was there? I don't think so. Jesus knew her beginning from her end and saw a need for a spiritual fulfillment. He was there at the right time to fill that emptiness in her and provide a way for eternal salvation. If we all could see through the eyes of Christ, this world would be a far better place for us to live.

PRAYER

Father, give us a heart of love and compassion like yours. Amen.

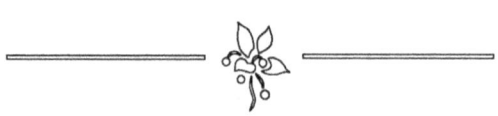

"In my distress I called to the Lord."

—2 SAMUEL 22:7 (NIV)

"IN MY DISTRESS I called out to the Lord; I called out to my God. From his temple he heard my voice; my cry came to his ears." He reached down from on high and rescued me, because He delighted in me. To the faithful, you show yourself faithful to the blameless you show yourself blameless, to the pure you show yourself pure, but to the devious you show yourself shrewd.

Lord, you are my lamp and you turn my darkness into light. As for God, His way is perfect, the Lord's Word is flawless, He shields all who takes refuge in Him. For who is God besides our Lord? And who is our rock besides God? It is God who arms me with strength, and teaches my hands to war, and my fingers to fight. The Lord lives, therefore I will sing praises to His name.

PRAYER

I will praise you for your faithfulness and love. Amen.

> *"Let your light so shine before men, that they may see your good works and glorify your Father in heaven."*

—MATTHEW 5:16

WE ARE NOT in this world alone, and there are many who are persecuted just for mentioning the name Jesus. The prayer of St. Francis of Assisi tells us how we can be ambassadors for Christ to bless others.

"Lord, make us an instrument of thy peace. Where there is hatred, let us sow love. Where there is despair, hope. Where there is darkness, light. Where there is doubt, faith. For it is in giving, that we receive. It is in pardoning, that we are pardoned. It is in dying, that we are born to eternal life."

Let us live our life in service to God and win souls for His kingdom. Blessings and love.

PRAYER

Hear our prayer, O Lord, that your light will shine through us. Amen.

"Behold, I lay in Zion a stone for a foundation."

—ISAIAH 28:16

JESUS IS THE stone that the builders have rejected, that has become the chief cornerstone. Salvation is found in no one else, for there is no other name under Heaven given to mankind by which we must be saved. The meaning of cornerstone is the rock on which the weight of the entire structure rests. Jesus is the Chief Cornerstone of our faith. This is what the Sovereign Lord says in Isaiah 28:16, "Behold, I lay in Zion a stone for a foundation, a tried stone, a precious cornerstone, a sure foundation; Whoever believes will not act hastily."

Our faith and trust stand in the rock of our salvation, Jesus Christ, who carries the weight of our sins and burdens, and He will never falter or lose His power.

PRAYER

Thank you for bearing our sins on the cross. Amen.

❚ "I am the Light of the world."

—JOHN 8:12

THERE ARE A lot of Bible verses that we can quote by heart. We have read them so much, until the words are easy to remember. For example, "I will never leave you nor forsake you" (Hebrews 13:5) and "Where I am, there you may be also" (John 14:3). But do you really understand the impact of these words that are spoken?

I'm quite sure most of us have seen the movie *Peter Pan*. When Peter found his shadow, he got a needle and thread and reconnected it to himself. Wherever there is light, you will always see your shadow. Now, think of the Light of God that's in you, and wherever you turn, that Light produces a shadow that never leaves you. Jesus is the Light of the world and He is attached to you, and is with you always, thus keeping His promise.

PRAYER

Thank you for being the light in my life that never goes out. Amen.

"Without faith it is impossible to please God."

—HEBREWS 11:6 (NIV)

THERE ARE SO many scriptures in the Bible that speaks of faith, that we must realize God is trying to let us know how important faith is. In my opinion, one of the most profound statements on faith is found in Hebrews 11, verse 6: "And without faith it is impossible to please God, because anyone who comes to him must believe that he exists and that he rewards those who earnestly seek him." We've learned that when we walk with God and do what pleases Him, He will be our "shield and reward" (Genesis 15:1). Everlasting life is a reward to all who turn to God in faith.

Ephesians 6, verse 16 tells us: "Take up the shield of faith, with which you can extinguish all the flaming arrows of the evil one." Faith isn't something that we can see in the natural, but our spiritual life depends on it. And our faith in God will break down any walls that separates us from Him.

PRAYER

Thank you for strengthening my faith that I never lose sight of you. Amen.

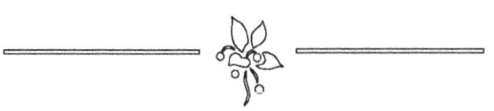

"Judge not, that ye be not judged."

—MATTHEW 7:1

WHETHER WE ADMIT it or not, we all make judgments either on people or situations. We encounter people throughout our lifetime, that by all standards, we considered to be good, and some, who we think are flawed by their actions against other human beings. But in the first two verses of Matthew 7, we are taught not to judge, or else we will be judged. For in the same manner we judge others, we will be judged, and with the same measure we use, it will be measured to us. Why do we look at the speck of sawdust which is in our brother's eye, and do not see the plank which is in our own eye?

None of us are perfect, and none of us should have a "holier than thou attitude." But we see others by our own standard of living and judge them accordingly. There is nothing that any of us can do to gain entry into the kingdom of God. It is a gift given to us by God's grace, through the sacrifice made by Jesus.

Think about it.

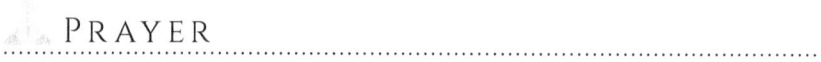

PRAYER

Give us eyes to see the good in people, as you see. Amen.

"Like newborn babies, crave pure spiritual milk, so that by it you may grow up in your salvation."

—1 PETER 2:2

HAVE YOU EVER had a desire to eat a specific food and couldn't get your hands on it right away and ate something you really didn't want? Then you come to find out that desire you had to begin with is still there. There is no substitute for the real thing because you won't be filled. It's the same way with the God's Word.

It is food for our soul, and nothing else will satisfy our need to be filled with more of Him, unless we drink God's spiritual water. In Hebrews 5, we learn that at a young age we are taught scriptures. We are basically spoon fed the Word until it becomes part of our life. As we mature, our need to be spiritually connected to God grows. The only way to satisfy that longing, is to come to know God through His Word. The revelation and enlightenment you receive will be well worth it.

PRAYER

Feed us with your Word, so that we may mature and godly wisdom. Amen.

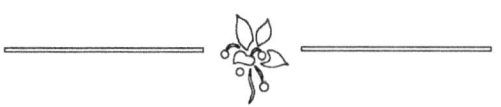

> *"Verily I say unto you, inasmuch as you did it unto the least of these My brethren, you did it to Me."*

—MATTHEW 25:40

WHAT WOULD WE be willing to do for Jesus Christ today? We go to church, and from the pastor on down, we have assignments to maintain our house of Worship, and to teach the Gospel of Jesus Christ, through the Word of God. But how effective has that been, in winning souls for God's kingdom?

We have willing workers in church, who cook, feed those who are hungry, provide clothes for people who are in need, and at the same time is spreading the good news of who God is. And never once are they looking for anything in return, except to bring glory to God. Matthew 25:40 tells us: "Assuredly, I say to you, inasmuch as you did it to one of the least of these My brethren, you did it to Me." Romans 10:17 says, "Faith comes by hearing, and hearing by the word of God." So, when we labor and speak God's Word at the same time, our labor is never in vain.

PRAYER

Thank you, Lord, that when we bless your people, it is never in vain. Amen.

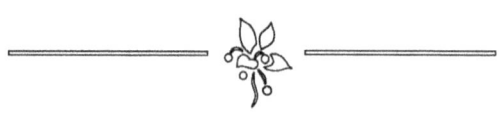

"Death and life are in the power of the tongue."

— PROVERBS 18:21

YOU HAVE HEARD it said that "death and life are in the power of the tongue" and "out of the abundance of the heart, the mouth speaks." Both of these are true. What we say out of our mouths we can't take back, so we should always be careful what we say. Words are powerful, and they carry a lot of weight. And whatever is truly in the deep recesses of our hearts, that's what comes out of our mouths. If we are born of God, His love is in us and every word that proceeds out of our mouths will be "yes" and "amen" and according to the will of God. We should all desire to have a heart like Christ, then we will be able to see others through His eyes and speak only that which is good.

PRAYER

Teach us to guard our words, that we will glorify your name. Amen.

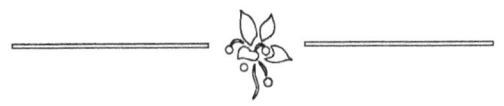

"Feed the hungry, and help those in trouble. Then your light will shine out from the darkness."

—ISAIAH 58:10 (NLT)

I HEARD ON the news that there was a young girl who was learning remotely and was crying. When the teacher asked why, she said because she was hungry. During the past three years, we have experienced situations that we never thought we would be in. But there is always enough food to go around that no child should ever be hungry. There was such an outpouring of love, compassion and donations, that this child and her family will never be hungry again.

The United States is one of the richest countries in the world and the bounty from God's land is enough to satisfy every living creature on the Earth. He is Jehovah Jirah, our Provider, and He will supply every need that we have out of the riches of His glory through Christ Jesus our Lord. Blessings to everyone who helps those in need.

PRAYER

Give us a heart of flesh to love and care for all people. Amen.

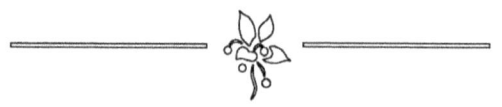

"Do not be anxious about anything, but in every situation, by prayer and petition, with thanksgiving, present your requests to God."

—PHILIPPIANS 4:6

I'VE GOTTEN INTO the habit of reading God's Word as though it was written specifically for me. God's Word is timeless and applies to situations that we face today. So, why do we lose sleep at night worrying about things that we really can't control? All worrying does, is bring on a multitude of health problems, and makes matters worse. Philippians 4:6–7 says, "Don't worry about anything, instead pray about everything. Tell God what you need and thank Him for all that He's done. Then you will experience God's peace, which exceeds anything we can understand. His peace will guard your hearts and minds, as you live in Christ Jesus." Faith is the substance of things hoped for, and the evidence of things not seen.

So, stand in faith and believe the work is already done, and God will never disappoint you.

PRAYER

Teach us through the power of the Holy Spirit to pray within your will. Amen.

‖ *"In the beginning God created the Heavens and the Earth."*

—GENESIS 1:1

ALL WE HAVE to do is turn on the TV, and we will see vehicles landing on Mars, or satellites going into the far reaches of the universe. We have gotten a glimpse of how vast space is, and the many galaxies and planets that it holds. And to coin a phrase, "Earth is just a drop in the bucket." When we put it all together, how can we not understand the unlimited power of God Almighty.

When we think about the planet that we live on, Earth, and we understand creation, everything that we have ever needed to sustain our life, God has given us. The animals to feed us, the fish in the sea, the fruits and vegetables that grow from the ground and the trees. Like a parent raises a child from birth, and gives the best of what they have, so has our Father given us His very best, capped off with unconditional love. And what He asks for in return, isn't too hard for any of us to do.

PRAYER

Help us to appreciate the best of everything you have given us. Amen.

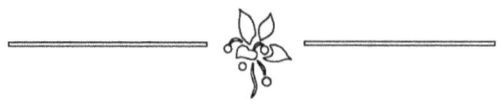

| *"Train up a child in the way he should go."*

—PROVERBS 22:6

IF YOU GREW up in a Christian home, come Sunday morning, as a family, we would all go to church together. As children, we attended Sunday school and learned about Jesus. And that was the beginning of our journey with Christ. Psalm 127:3 tells us that "children are a heritage from the LORD, the fruit of the womb is a reward." Children are a gift entrusted to us by God to raise in glory to His name. And we do our best to instill in our children all that we have learned that is good and right. But from the time they are born, it's an uphill battle because of the desires of this world. But Proverbs 22:6 says, "Train up a child in the way he should go, and when he is old he will not depart from it."

Plant the seed, and God will cause it to increase and bear good fruit.

PRAYER

Father, plant the seed of your Word in us that we may grow in righteousness. Amen.

67

‖ *"If we walk in the light, as He is in the light."*

−1 JOHN 1:7

GOD IS LIGHT and in Him there is no darkness. If we say that we are children of God, then there can't be any darkness in us because light and dark cannot exist in the same place. If we walk in the light, as Christ is in the light, then we can fellowship with one another and the Blood of Jesus purifies us from all sin. If the truth is in us, then we cannot say that we are without sin, because we would only be fooling ourselves.

If we confess our sins, God is faithful and just and we will be forgiven and cleansed of all unrighteousness. If we claim we have not sinned, then we are making God out to be a liar and His Word is not in us. But if anyone does sin, we have an Advocate with the Father, Jesus Christ the Righteous One. He is the atoning sacrifice for our sins, and not for ours only but for the sins of the whole world.

PRAYER

Thank you, Jesus, that your Word removes the stain of sin from us. Amen.

68

"Watch out for false prophets. They come to you in sheep's clothing, but inwardly are ferocious wolves."

—MATTHEW 7:15 (NIV)

I'M SURE AT one time or another we have heard the phrase "A wolf in sheep's clothing." I don't think I'd be wrong in saying that some of us have met people who are just like that. These are people who are grumblers and backbiters. They are selfish and follow their own evil desires. They boast about themselves and follow others to use them for their own advantage.

But we are God's holy people and once the Word of God is established in us, we can recognize the tactics used by others and unbelievers who try to infiltrate our faith and turn our hearts away from God. These are ungodly people who pervert the grace of God into a license for immorality to deny the existence of Jesus Christ. But as true Christians, we have godly wisdom and greater is He who is in us than he who is in this world.

PRAYER

Lord, teach us to recognize people who pervert your Word for their own benefit. Amen.

"Let this mind be in you which is also in Christ Jesus."

—PHILIPPIANS 2:5

WHEN WE WERE little, if someone asked us what we wanted to be when we grew up, the usual response would be a fireman, policeman, a doctor or a nurse. But no one ever said *I want to be just like Jesus.*

As we got older and learned more about who Jesus is, our answers are much different now. God is amazing and wanting to be like Jesus comes out of most Christians mouth's now. Imagine if we could have a heart like Jesus, full of love for all people that we don't speak bad about anyone, that we encourage people through love and we don't destroy by our words. Wouldn't our lives be more blessed? If we could possess part of Christ's divine nature and heal physical sicknesses by a touch or a word, how much of a blessing would we be? Remember that with God, all things are possible.

PRAYER

Father, transform us into the image of Jesus Christ, that we will be more like Him. Amen.

70

│ *"Look at the birds in the air, for they neither sow nor reap."*

—MATTHEW 6:26

WE HAVE LEARNED that every good and perfect gift comes from our Father above. But have we ever stopped to think what that really means? It means that whatever we need to sustain us here in this life, God has provided. Everything that we have ever been given—the clothes we wear, the food we eat, the devices we use to stay connected—was provided by our God.

Matthew 6:26 says, "Look at the birds in the air, they neither sow nor reap or store in barns, and yet, our heavenly Father feeds them. Aren't we much more valuable than they are?" Our God wants us to receive the best He has to offer, and He will give it to all whose hearts are turned to Him.

PRAYER
···

Thank you, Lord, that you have given us everything to have a bountiful life in this land. Amen.

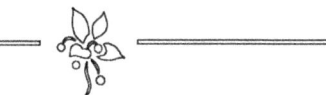

"God created man in His own image."

— GENESIS 1:27

LATELY, I'VE BEEN going through some challenges, that frankly, have just worn me out. And I sat here trying to find a remedy for this, a pill for that, to try and ease what I was going through in my body. But I will be honest, if I could've gotten my foot high enough, I would've kicked myself, because I know better. And when you know better, you do better. I had to remind myself that God created me, and He knows every inch of my body. And I had to repent and turn to God and ask for His divine solution.

Why was I thinking that I could do better than what God could do?

God has a solution for every problem, physically spiritually and financially. So now, using the wisdom He gave me, I have placed everything in God's hands, and wait patiently for His divine help. That's something we all need to do, because the battle is not ours, it's the Lord's.

PRAYER

Thank you, Father, for being the healer of all of our sicknesses. Amen.

"Though I speak with the tongues of men and of angels, but have not love, I have become sounding brass or a clanging cymbal."

—1 CORINTHIANS 13:1

IF WE HAVE the gift of prophecy, and can fathom all mysteries and knowledge, and have faith that can move mountains, but do not have love, we are nothing. If we give all we possess to the poor, but do not have love, we gain nothing.

Love is patient and kind; it doesn't boast and is not proud. Love does not delight in evil but rejoices in truth. Love never fails, and when we were children, we behaved like children. But now we are grown we put all those childish things behind us. God is pure love, and we were made in His image. So, when we look in the mirror, we should see God's reflection in us.

PRAYER

Thank you, Jesus, that we have grown in your love that extends to others. Amen.

"Let love be without hypocrisy. Abhor what is evil. Cling to what is good."

—ROMANS 12:9

PHYSICALLY, WE LIVE in this world, but as we are being changed into the image of Christ, our interest in this world becomes less and less, as we mature in the things of God. Our goal is not to remain on this Earth because it is run by Satan and his crew. But daily as we abhor what is evil and cling to what is good, we are renewed in our body, mind, soul and spirit into the image of Christ.

Think of Earth as a weigh station that checks the baggage that you picked up from your life here. Before you can move on, you have to leave behind that excess baggage that is weighing you down. When you enter the kingdom of heaven, you can't take anything from this Earth with you. Remember, this world is not our home, we are just passing through.

PRAYER

Thank you, Lord, that you change us daily to be more like you. Amen.

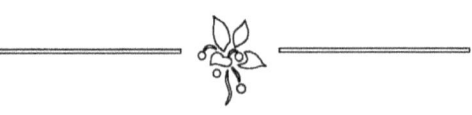

*"And you He made alive, who were
dead in trespasses and sins."*

—EPHESIANS 2:1

DID YOU KNOW that many people could be physically alive, but spiritually dead? In Ephesians 2:1, we learn that we were dead in our transgressions and sins. But God, in His great mercy, has made us alive in Christ. God gives life to the dead, and He will give life to our mortal bodies, because of His Spirit who lives in us. Before Jesus ascended into heaven, He told His followers to remain in Jerusalem until the gift of the Father, the Holy Spirit, was given to them.

On the day of Pentecost, the Spirit of God came upon them like tongues of fire, and they were able to speak in different languages. Unless Christ had ascended to His Father, the Holy Spirit would not have come to be with us to this very day. This is a gift from God, and the power of His Spirit is working in us, that we are called the children of God.

PRAYER

Thank you for the gift of your Holy Spirit that teaches us all things. Amen.

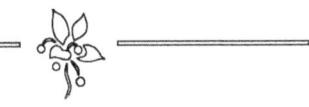

"All scripture is God-breathed and is useful for teaching, rebuking, correcting and training in righteousness, so that the servant of God may be thoroughly equipped for every good work."

—2 TIMOTHY 3:16-17 (NIV)

MOST PEOPLE WHO own a car have GPS on it. And it is very useful, especially when they're not sure of where they're going. GPS will put them at the right place.

That is how I see the Word of God.

He has given us knowledge, from before time began, of who He is and His power that is eternal. God has also given us examples for us to see how lives were blessed because of faith and obedience, but also what happens when He was disobeyed. God has given us everything that we need to have a fruitful, blessed and prosperous life, when we acknowledge His holiness and walk in faith, subjective to His will. And even though we were born in sin, through salvation by Jesus Christ, we have been handed the keys to the kingdom of heaven.

Let's make sure we don't lose those keys.

PRAYER

Thank you, Jesus, that your Word teaches us to live in spirit and in truth. Amen.

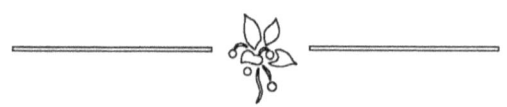

76

"No temptation has overtaken you except what is common to mankind."

—1 CORINTHIANS 10:13 (NIV)

MANY OF US don't realize that the things we do every day, our daily routine, has subjected us to trials and temptations without us even knowing it. As Christians, daily we do our best to be more like Christ, but there's always some little thing we don't even think about, that separates us from God. But God knows our frame, He remembers that we are dust.

1 Corinthians 10, verse 13 tells us: "No temptation has overtaken us except what is common to mankind; and God is faithful, and He will not allow us to be tempted beyond what we are able, but with the temptation will provide the way of escape also, so that we will be able to endure it." How great is His love for us, that He always provides a way.

PRAYER

We praise you for giving us a way for true repentance. Amen.

77

"Who can straighten what he has made crooked?"

—ECCLESIASTES 7:13 (NIV)

KING SOLOMON WAS a man blessed by God and was rich in wisdom. He studied people and situations and was wise in encouraging others, to enlighten them to truth and folly. He has found that "God created mankind upright, but they have gone in search of many schemes" (Ecclesiastes 7:29, NIV). No matter how hard we try to do what is right, we all fall short of the glory of God. The heart, above all else, is desperately wicked. And who can know it but God. Seeking and having wisdom is a good thing; it is a shelter and preserves those who have it.

Consider all the things God has done: Who can straighten what He has made crooked? And who can discover anything about their future? Indeed, there is no one on this Earth who is righteous, no one who does what is right and never sins. When we can gain understanding, through knowledge of who God is, that is the beginning of wisdom that we should all pursue after.

PRAYER

Thank you, Father, that we find safety in the wisdom of your Word. Amen.

"Trust in the Lord with all your heart."

—PROVERBS 3:5 (NIV)

WE ARE FACED with making decisions every day. Some choices are more important than others, but nonetheless, they require an answer. We can reach out to others for their opinions, but the final decision is always ours to make. But Proverbs 3:5–6 tells us, "Trust in the Lord with all your heart and lean not on your own understanding. But in all your ways acknowledge Him, and He will direct your path." Our faithfulness should never leave us. We must keep it with us always. It will be health and prosperity to us because we look to the Lord for all things.

We might follow the advice of our friends, but a lot of times you'll find yourself falling into a ditch, that you can't climb out of. But God will never steer you wrong, He'll give you the best advice and path to take.

PRAYER

Your advice never steers us wrong, and we praise you, Lord. Amen.

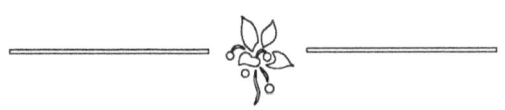

"For her proceeds are better than the profits
of silver, and her gain than fine gold."

—PROVERBS 3:14

WHEN WE HAVE received the baptism of the Holy Spirit, no possession we have seems that important anymore. We can consider the things we have gained in this world as garbage, because nothing can surpass the knowledge of Christ Jesus in our life. We don't put any confidence in the flesh, and we don't have any righteousness of our own, but through Christ, our righteousness comes from God based on our faith. Our desire is to know more about Jesus, and be more like Him, and come to know the power of His resurrection. So, "Forgetting what is behind, and straining toward what is ahead, we must press toward the goal to win the prize, for which God has called us Heavenward in Christ Jesus" (1 Corinthians 3:13–14).

 PRAYER
....

Increase our faith to keep our eyes focused on you, Lord God. Amen.

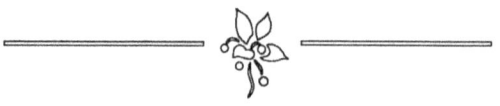

"No weapon formed against you shall prosper."

—ISAIAH 54:17

WE SHOULD ALWAYS be careful who we associate with because there are many wolves out there in sheep's clothing. People will always look at what you have, and a jealous streak will rise up in them because they're not content with their own possessions or life. But the Lord tells us, "No weapons formed against you will prosper, and every tongue which rises against you in judgment, the Lord will condemn. This is the heritage of the servants of the Lord" (Isaiah 54:17).

There may be many enemies that rise up against us. But the Lord is a shield around us, our glory, the one who lifts up our head. And when we call out to the Lord, He answers us. When we're asleep or awake, the Lord sustains us. We don't have to worry what people do or say about us because the hand of the Lord is always with us and delivers us.

PRAYER

Thank you that you watch over us day and night to keep us safe from all harm and evil. Amen.

"The Lord will fight for you, you need only to be still."

—EXODUS 14:14 (NIV)

I CAN HONESTLY say that there are a lot of people who have made it their profession to complain about every little thing. In Exodus 14, God delivered the people of Israel from Egyptian slavery and because they saw the Red Sea in front of them and Pharaoh's chariots behind them, they were ready to kill Moses. Once again, Moses had to remind them of the power of God that they witnessed so many times before. "Do not be afraid. Stand firm and see the deliverance the Lord will bring you today . . . The Lord will fight for you, you need only to be still" (Exodus 14:13–14). Then, the Red Sea parted.

All we have to do is be still and know that He is God. And there isn't anything that God will not do for the people He loves, and who walk in faith, according to His Word. We have to remember that God is alive and His Word is still working on our behalf.

PRAYER

We place all of our battles in your hands for the victory. Amen.

"Do not be afraid, nor be dismayed; be strong and of good courage, for thus the Lord will do to all your enemies against whom you fight."

—JOSHUA 10:25

BEFORE THE DEATH of Moses, Joshua was anointed to carry on the work started by Moses, to fulfill the promises of God. Joshua was a man of faith and walked in total obedience to Jehovah God. He was a warrior and commanded a mighty army of Israelites to do battle, and the Lord was always with him. In Joshua 10:25, the Lord encouraged him: "Do not be afraid of your enemy, I have given them into your hand. None of them will be able to withstand you."

Joshua never doubted the word spoken by God and walked with complete confidence. In one battle, he needed more time to defeat and pursue the enemy. Before this, Joshua said to the Lord in the presence of Israel: "Sun, stand still over Gibeon, and you, Moon, over the valley of Aijalon" (Joshua 10:12). The sun stopped and delayed going down for about a full day.

This is the perfect example to show all of us, that when our faith and obedience lines up with the will of God, He will honor the words we speak.

PRAYER

Teach us to be obedient to your will through your Word. Amen.

*"And they stood and confessed their sins,
and the iniquities of their fathers."*

—NEHEMIAH 9:2

MANY FAMILIES ARE plagued by generational curses and don't even know it. But once you get to the root of the problem, these curses can be broken and stopped in their tracks. In Nehemiah 9, we see where people came together fasting and praying, not only for their sins, but for the sins that their ancestors had committed, for God to wipe the slate clean. They spent a good part of the day confessing and worshiping.

God doesn't hold grudges, and as long as there is true repentance, our sins will be forgiven. If the mouth of the Lord declared it, He will fulfill His promise. The glorious name of our God must be exalted from everlasting to everlasting because He gives life to everything. When we please our God, He will make His face to shine on us forever.

PRAYER

Thank you that you are a loving, forgiving God, who has placed our sins behind us. Amen.

> *"Do you not know that you are the temple of God and that the Spirit of God dwells in you?"*

—1 CORINTHIANS 3:16

IF YOU TAKE a jar or a bottle, and fill it with water, the water will take on the shape of the container it is in. Likewise, when we read God's Word, there is an infilling of the Holy Spirit that will consume every part of our body. It will not change what is on the outside, but what is inside of us.

Our flesh is our worst enemy, and nothing really can be done to change our sin-riddled bodies. But the power of the Holy Spirit can "create in us a clean heart and renew the spirit inside of us" to make us line up in obedience to the Word of God. Isaiah 29:13 says, "These people come to me with their mouths and honor me with their lips, but their hearts are far from me." So, if a heart change is what is needed, pray and ask God to make that change in you and He will gladly oblige.

PRAYER

Almighty God, teach us to line up with your will, by the power of your Spirit. Amen.

"Who is a God like you, who pardons sin and forgives the transgression of the remnant of his inheritance? You do not stay angry forever but delight to show mercy."

—MICAH 7:18 (NIV)

FROM THE TIME of the fall in the Garden of Eden, God saw man's inhumanity to man. We serve a God of second chances and He gave His people a way to atone for their sin. Sacrifices of different animals were made according to the extent of their sins and was accepted by God in atonement. But people's hearts would turn back to a sinful nature and forget their promises to God.

It was a hopeless situation and our only hope was an eternal sacrifice that couldn't be undone—the sacrificial Lamb of God that takes away the sins of the world. Jesus poured out His life unto death and was numbered with the transgressors. Like a lamb, He was led to the slaughter and He opened not His mouth, but willingly carried our sins to the cross.

What a Mighty God we serve!

PRAYER

Thank you, Father, that your forgiveness is for all who believe in your Son. Amen.

"I saw the holy city, the new Jerusalem,
coming down out of heaven from God."

—REVELATION 21:2

I'VE BEEN TO the eye doctor and I've had my pupils dilated. When I've walked back outside, every color that I saw was the brightest, most beautiful colors I have ever seen. I remember thinking that this must be what Heaven is like - everything bright and beautiful. But God has given us a peek into the beauty of His kingdom.

John 14:2 tells of the mansions that Christ has prepared for us when He comes to receive us unto Himself. Hebrews 12:22 describes Mt. Zion, the heavenly Jerusalem and city of our living God, where we will worship with untold blessings. We have gone on vacations and seen some of God's most beautiful creations. But nothing can ever compare to the beauty of God's holiness, streets of gold, beautiful precious gemstones and standing in the presence of Jesus our Savior.

PRAYER

Thank you that the old things have passed away, and all things will become new. Amen.

| *"For where two or three are gathered in my name."*

—MATTHEW 18:20

AS THE BODY of Christ, it's good that we worship and fellowship together. Colossians 3:16-17 says, "Let the message of Christ dwell among you richly as you teach and admonish one another with all wisdom through Psalms, hymns, and songs from the Spirit, singing to God with gratitude in your hearts. And whatever you do, whether in word or deed, do it all in the name of the Lord Jesus, giving thanks to God the Father through Him."

True worship becomes a habit and a lifestyle that we maintain. Of course, you can worship God by word or deed on your own, but God's presence manifests where His people gather together to magnify His name. Matthew 18:20 says, "For where two or three are gathered in My name, there I will be among them."

We all benefit when we come together as one body and worship our God. His blessings will be poured in us because of our obedience, and by His grace.

PRAYER

Thank you for bringing us together to worship your majesty. Amen.

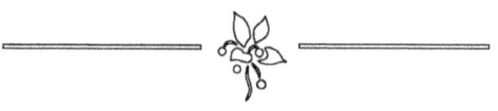

> *"For wisdom is better than rubies, and all the things one may desire cannot be compared with her."*

—PROVERBS 8:11

WISDOM IS THE principle thing. Seek godly wisdom and above everything else, gain an understanding of God's Word through knowledge. God is alive and so is His Word and it is sharper than any double-edged sword. When we read it and digest it, it works on the inside of us to separate the good from the bad.

Pray and ask God, by the power of His Word, to remove whatever is unclean, unholy and unrighteous from in us and to fill us with the light of God that drives out all darkness. As the seed of Abraham and the righteousness of God, we can be vessels used by God to fulfill His desires and will on this Earth. We are transformed body, mind, soul and spirit into new creations that we don't conform to anything in this world but are transformed by the renewing of our mind. We are faith walkers, and our faith stands not in the wisdom of men, but in the power of God.

PRAYER

Thank you, Lord, that the wisdom of your Word gives meaning to our life. Amen.

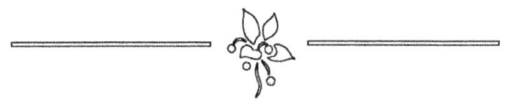

"Who is a God like you, who pardons sin and forgives the transgression of the remnant of his inheritance? You do not stay angry forever but delight to show mercy."

—PSALM 46:1 (NIV)

LIFE HAS CHANGED so much that we're not even sure what normal is anymore. But as in all things, we make adjustments to maintain a healthy lifestyle. Everyone was scrambling to get the COVID vaccine, but even that initially proved to be a difficulty. Hospitalizations are down, but we are encouraged to still wear masks, even though it's deemed unnecessary. It seems as though the more we try to fix things, the further away we get from a solution. But there is a light not only at the end of the tunnel, but a light inside, to drive away all the darkness that we've been going through.

His name is Jesus.

Where He is, no darkness can exist.

With Jesus as part of our life, everything is bearable. God didn't say that our life would be easy, but that He would make all things possible. But just bear in mind that with everything we're going through, Jesus is fulfilling His promise to never leave us. He's helping us carry our burdens.

Jesus, our shelter in the storm.

PRAYER

I praise you, Lord, for you are always by my side to the good and bad. Amen.

"For where your treasure is, there your heart will be also."

—MATTHEW 6:21 (NIV)

WHAT IS IT that you value in life, that you will spend your time, energy and money on? Most people will spend their time on things that make them comfortable and bring joy to them and their families. But in Matthew 6:21 Christ tells us that "where your treasure is, there your heart will be also." He teaches us to treasure things that will last forever, and last for an eternity and not fade away. "Do not lay up for yourselves treasures on earth, where rust and moth destroy and where thieves break in and steal; but lay up for yourselves treasures in heaven" (Matthew 6:19–20).

The eye is the lamp of the body. So, if you keep your eyes focused on the light, that is in Christ Jesus, that is where your heart will be also.

PRAYER

Let our hearts stay connected to you, to reap in the benefits of your glory. Amen.

"Sanctity them by Your truth. Your word is truth."

—JOHN 17:17

IF WE ARE made in the image of God, shouldn't we have the same characteristics as our Father?

God is love.

Anyone who wants to be like Jesus should possess a love that is genuine and pure. But being citizens of this world puts us in a difficult position. You will run into people who will do their best to rub you the wrong way, just to cause friction because of their own insecurities or problems. But when you have made Christ the center of your life, you are no longer citizens of this world, but of the kingdom of Heaven. We look to God for wisdom on how to deal with these difficult situations. A soft tongue turns away wrath and showing love can conquer all.

PRAYER

Let your Word purify and cleanse our hearts to follow after you. Amen.

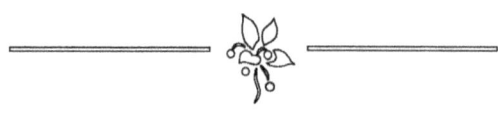

"Present your bodies a living sacrifice, holy, acceptable to God, which is your reasonable service. And do not be conformed to this world, but be transformed by the renewing of your mind, that you may prove what is that good and acceptable and perfect will of God."

—ROMANS 12:1-2

WE ARE NOT lambs or goats to be sacrificed to God. But the acts of service and sacrifice we give of our time in doing what we can to help others is doing the work of the Lord.

We must live with love for each other as God has taught us. Whatever we do must come from our hearts with a willingness of spirit. God has already given us everything that we need, including His grace and salvation. So, let's honor Him with an attitude of gratitude and thanksgiving.

PRAYER

Give us a heart for service to you, by loving and serving other others. Amen.

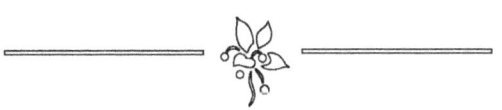

93

> *"He is your praise, and He is your God, who has done for you these great and awesome things which your eyes have seen."*

—DEUTERONOMY 10:21

HAVE YOU EVER experienced a miracle in your life?

By definition, a miracle is an extraordinary event that cannot be reasonably explained. In the Bible, we've read about miraculous occurrences like the parting of the Red Sea, the birth of Jesus, Jesus giving sight to the blind and healing broken and diseased bodies. A lot of people think that because we go through so much suffering, pain and diseases in our bodies today that God has stopped performing miracles. That could not be further from the truth.

God is very active in our lives and can supernaturally manifest what we need when we need it. Haven't you ever prayed and have your prayers answered? When your prayers and your faith lines up with the Word of God, you will see the hand of God move in your life. Don't keep looking for the Red Sea to be parted because the smallest blessings are miracles from God too.

PRAYER

Thank you, Jesus, that when we awake in the morning, that is our first miracle of the day. Amen.

> *"To give them beauty for ashes, the oil of joy for mourning, the garment of praise for the spirit of heaviness."*

—ISAIAH 61:3

WHEN WE SING songs of praise and worship to our God, we are inviting Him to change the very atmosphere in our life. It's as though the Ruash, (the wind of God), is blowing through our bodies, and removing everything that prevents the Spirit of God from fully taking over in us. In church, when the choir sings, the words and music strikes a cord deep within us, and tears will flow because it speaks to us personally. At that point, we feel a more intimate connection with our God.

Music is a wonderful way to express how we feel, when we lift our voice in praise and thanksgiving to our Lord. That's when we will receive beauty for ashes, the oil of joy for mourning, and a garment of praise for the spirit of heaviness. Then we will feel, "It is well with my soul."

PRAYER

Lord, always let us keep praise on our lips and thanksgiving in our hearts for all of your goodness and mercy. Amen.

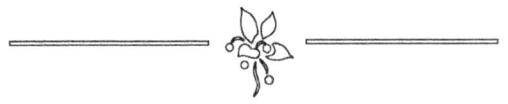

"But those who hope in the Lord will renew their strength."

—ISAIAH 40:31 (NIV)

HOW MANY OF you have ever stood in front of a crowd of people, and was so nervous, you could hardly speak? Or being so fearful when taking a test, because you were unsure of the answers you would give? Well, just to remind you, fear and doubt is the devils playground. He will attack you in areas that you feel weak in. "But when we trust in the Lord, we will renew our strength. We will run and not get weary, we will walk and not faint" (Isaiah 40:31).

In areas that we are lacking, the Lord will pick us up. In Exodus 4, verse 11, The Lord tells us, "Who gave human beings their mouth? Who makes them deaf or mute? Who gives them sight or makes them blind? Is it not I, the Lord?" The Lord is always there for us when we need Him the most. So don't ever think you're out there on your own, the Lord goes with you wherever you go.

PRAYER

Thank you, Lord, that you are always by our side, and we wait patiently for your help. Amen.

"May my prayer be set before you like incense; may the lifting up of my hands be like the evening sacrifice."

— PSALM 141:2 (NIV)

THERE IS UNSPEAKABLE joy and a calmness of spirit that we experience when we develop a close relationship with our God. Knowing that God is with us all the time brings a security and peace to our soul. So, we don't have to be anxious about anything. However, in every situation by prayer and supplication, with thanksgiving, we can present our petitions to God and the peace of God which surpasses all of our understanding will guard our hearts and minds in Christ Jesus.

Many of us never grew up with a silver spoon in our mouths. So, we know what it's like to have and we've also experienced lack. But through it all, we were always happy because, God has supplied all of our needs according to His riches in glory. We have learned that we can do all things through Christ who gives us strength.

God supplies all of our needs.

PRAYER

Lord, out of the abundance of your grace and mercy, you have given us everything to live a fruitful life. Amen.

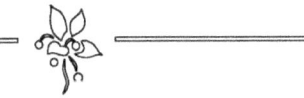

"Where can I go from Your Spirit? Or where can I flee from Your presence?"

—PSALM 139:7

WHEN YOU HAVE come to know the voice of the Lord and He points you in a direction to go, you have no choice but to obey. Just like Jonah, you can run but you cannot hide. Where on this Earth can you go that the Lord's eye is not on you?

We should never judge a person "for the Lord doesn't see as man sees; for man looks at the outward appearance, but the Lord looks at the heart." When an anointing is placed on your life by God, He will cause even your enemies to be at peace with you. When the anointing of the Holy Spirit is placed on your life, you have no choice but to do what God has called you to do.

PRAYER

Lord, keep my heart pure that I may not look down on others. Amen.

"You will seek Me and find Me when you seek Me with all your heart."

—JEREMIAH 29:13 (NIV)

BECAUSE OF THE Lord's great love we are not consumed, for His compassions never fail. They are new every morning, great is your faithfulness, Lord, unto us. As undeserving as we are, the Lord has made a way for us to be saved, through the sacrifice of His Son, Jesus Christ. God has declared His plans for us, to prosper us and give us a hope and a future. Then when we call on Him, and go and pray to Him, He will listen.

When we seek Him, we will find Him, when we seek Him with all our hearts. He will give wisdom to the wise and knowledge to the discerning. God will reveal deep and hidden things, because He knows what lies in the darkness, and all light dwells in Him.

PRAYER

Thank you, Lord, that you are faithful, and never far from us. Amen.

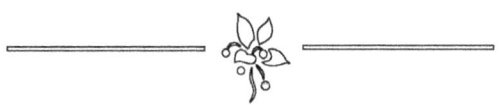

ABOUT THE AUTHOR

Sandra was born and raised in New York City, where she lives to this day. She graduated from City College of New York with a BA in philosophy. She has been a member of St. Paul's Progressive Methodist Church for over half a century and is a Bible teacher of the Word of God. In humility and love, she gives all praise, honor, and glory to Almighty God and our Lord Jesus for her walk of faith that increases every day.

May the Lord bless and keep you all as you strive to enter His glorious kingdom.